Copyright © 2018 Patrick A. Hegarty.

All rights reserved. No part of this publication may be reproduced, distributed or transmitted in any form or by any means, including photocopying, recording, or other electronic or mechanical methods, without the prior written permission of Patrick Hegarty, except in the case of brief quotations embodied in critical reviews and certain other noncommercial uses permitted by copyright law. For permission requests, email the author, with subject line "Attention: Permissions Enquiry" at the email address below.

info@hegarty.com.au

www.hegarty.com.au

Scriptures quoted from: New International Version of the Bible. Scripture taken from the Holy Bible, NEW INTERNATIONAL VERSION®. Copyright ©1973, 1978, 1984 International Bible Society. All rights reserved throughout the world. Used by permission of International Bible Society.

Scripture quotations identified MSG are from The Message. Copyright © 1993, 1994, 1995 by Eugene Peterson. Used by permission of NavPress Publishing Group.

Any internet addresses (websites, blogs, etc.) in this book are offered as a resources. They are not intended in any way to be or imply an endorsement by Patrick Hegarty, nor does Patrick Hegarty vouch for the content of these sites for the life of this book.

Contents

Using the Daily Journal & Workbook v

Group Session – (INTRODUCTIONS) 1

Group Session – (HOW ARE YOU DOING?) 5

    [1.1] Come to life 6

    [1.2] Called 8

    [1.3] What owns you? 10

    [1.4] Afraid and alone 16

    [1.5] Corrupted comparison 18

    [1.6] Redeemed hope 20

Group Session – (WHAT DO YOU WANT?) 21

    [2.1] Out of the box 22

    [2.2] The posture of hope 24

    [2.3] Building desire 26

    [2.4] Desiring God 28

    [2.5] Desiring freedom 30

    [2.6] Creating a hope 32

Group Session – (KAIROS) 35

    [3.1] What time is it? 38

    [3.2] One more night 40

    [3.3] Spotting the problem 42

    [3.4] Approaching the no-go zone 44

    [3.5] What is the alternative? 46

    [3.6] Placing everything on the table 48

Group Session – (REPENT) **49**

[4.1] A rhythm of grace 50

[4.2] Repentance 52

[4.3] Looking behind the idol 54

[4.4] Dishonour 56

[4.5] Offence 58

[4.6] Navigating a turn 60

Group Session – (BELIEVE) **61**

[5.1] The kingdom is at hand 62

[5.2] What storm? 64

[5.3] The rest of faith 66

[5.4] Pathway to joy 68

[5.5] The higher calling 70

[5.6] A point of no return 72

Group Session – (WALKING IT OUT) **75**

[6.1] What am I aiming for, really? 76

[6.2] Walking in union 78

[6.3] Heart of flesh, face like flint 80

[6.4] How did Jesus grow people? 82

[6.5] Form a strategy 84

[6.6] Take a step 86

Appendix 1: A Plan to Change 87

Notes from your Retreat 90

Using the Daily Journal & Workbook

This Daily Journal & Workbook is a companion of the book *re:FORM*.

In the hardcopy, at the end of each chapter of the book, a response question is asked which assists you in the personal application of the principles mentioned.

This journal provides an easy way to log your responses in order, and have quick access to them during small group meetings.

FOR USE AS A DAILY JOURNAL

Each chapter of the book has a dedicated section in this workbook. Simply look up the appropriate chapter number in the Contents section, and write down your thoughts and responses.

FOR USE AS A SMALL GROUP WORKBOOK

If you are working through this material as a group, there are Group Session notes included to guide your discussion. The Daily Journal pages are sandwiched within these group sessions to ensure easy reference to your responses during group meetings.

[INTRODUCTIONS]

Group Session 1

Spend some time going around the group, hearing the names, family details and life context of each participant.

Q. What would you like to get from this course?

_____

_____

ABOUT RE:FORM

READ TOGETHER:

Welcome to re:FORM. This course is all about equipping you to become what the apostle Paul called the spiritual person (1 Corinthians 3:1; Greek: *pneumatikos*).

The great majority of Christians believe they are spiritually mature but, in reality, experience little of the empowering presence of God in their daily lives. We don't become mature simply by doing the Christian life for years, or by behaving like a nice person.

Being a spiritual person is about living with the power of God working through us, activated in an intimate and dynamic relationship with our God. 1 Corinthians 4:20 confirms that the *"kingdom of God is not a matter of talk, but of power"*.

Becoming spiritual seldom happens by accident. To grow, we need to engage with God through a deliberate rhythm of grace called "Repentance and Belief". This material will equip you to do just that. You will be able to identify an area of your life where you need the Spirit's help to overcome, and to work through the process to being spirit-empowered.

HOW TO GO THROUGH MATERIAL:

There are six daily readings per week to process and respond to. Do one per day only, as you will need to meditate on and process the concepts slowly. Fill in the Your response section slowly, reflectively and honestly, or you won't receive the full benefit of the process.

In your group meetings your facilitator will help you process and apply the week's concepts.

GROUP AGREEMENT

For your group to be safe and effective, you will need to agree on how you will interact and honour each other. Talk through together which boundaries you may want to have in place for the duration of the course. Below are some suggestions and you can add your own.

GROUP ATTENDANCE

We will honour each other by being on time and regularly attending meetings.

SAFE ENVIRONMENT

We will create a place where each person is protected and loved, free to share without judgment or unsolicited advice.

RESPECT DIFFERENCES

We will be gentle and gracious to those with different spiritual maturity, opinions and temperaments.

CONFIDENTIALITY

What is said in the group stays in the group.

FAITHFULNESS

We will diligently engage with the material, processing our responses honestly.

OTHER POINTS OF IMPORTANCE

_____

_____

_____

YOUR SPIRITUAL JOURNEY SO FAR

Q: Can you describe what it is like for you to be empowered by God's Spirit in some area of your life?

_____

_____

_____

Q. What is an area where you have seen the most obvious change in your life since you met Christ?

_____

_____

Q. What factors contributed to that transformation?

_____

_____

_____

Q. If you could identify a few key things that have incited you to grow spiritually, what would they be?

_____

_____

_____

_____

_____

Q. Might there have been a better or more effective way to grow in that area?

_____

_____

_____

_____

Pray for Each Other

Take some time discussing the prayer needs of each person in the group and how best you will support them this week.

Week 1 – How are you doing?

Group Session 2

Use this section at the beginning your 2nd group meeting.

INTRODUCTION

The first group of readings (1.1 through 1.6) shone a light on the contrasting vision that both Jesus and Satan have for your life.

Jesus offers you abundance and freedom, while Satan is intent on destroying your destiny in Christ.

The thief comes only to steal and kill and destroy; I have come that they may have life, and have it to the full. (John 10:10)

Q. What was your overall response to the first week of teaching?

_____

_____

_____

Discuss together your responses from this week's teaching:

[1.1]

Come to life

CHAPTER SUMMARY:

- You are designed to be with God.
- You are not truly alive unless His breath is helping you live.
- A spiritual believer is one who is living from the Spirit of God.

YOUR RESPONSE:

Q. What is your response to this offer of life? Is this what you want? Do you yearn for relief from the agendas of this world and the need to do well or look good? Spend a few minutes writing down your response and desire for God at the beginning of this course. At the end, things may well look very different for you.

_____

_____

_____

_____

_____

_____

_____

[1.2]

Called

CHAPTER SUMMARY:

- Your calling is primarily to become the person God has made you to be.
- God doesn't want less of you, He wants all of you.
- God doesn't want you dead, He wants you to be fully alive.

YOUR RESPONSE:

Q. What has God been dealing with in your life? Does any area continually come up as a problem? If you had to guess, what do you think you need to put to death so you can fully live?

_____

_____

_____

_____

_____

_____

_____

_____

[1.3]
What owns you?

CHAPTER SUMMARY:

- We often have slave-drivers which compel us to react.
- Our idea of "doing fine" is quite different to God's ideal.
- Simply trying harder to overcome inner pain doesn't work.

YOUR RESPONSE:

Read Exodus 3:7–8

1. God hears the cry of those who are controlled by negative influences and wants to bring freedom.

2. **Spiritual Health Assessment** (from next page).
   Fill in the survey slowly and honestly, looking to identify some of the common areas (or slave drivers) in which many past participants of this material have found significant transformation.

3. Then reflect here on the following:

What is the most consistent issue that you battle with in life, that you know is holding you back or limiting your spiritual growth?

_____

Q. Is there a particular fear, addiction, relational dysfunction, shame or other consistent issue that you struggle to control? What is it that you consistently do that you know is not God's plan for you? _____

Spiritual Health Assessment

PART 1: SPIRITUAL & EMOTIONAL MATURITY

Spiritual maturity is measured by our ability to follow the leadings of the Holy Spirit within us, and live from the nature and priority of Christ. In the following areas, indicate how you rate out of 10, and at the end of this course you will re-visit this assessment to see if you have grown.

1. I am aware daily of the Spirit's tangible help in my thoughts and actions

As I begin this book		On finishing this book	
I rate myself at:	My friend/spouse says:	I rate myself at:	My friend/spouse says:

2. I am aware of and operate in the gifts of the Spirit fairly consistently

As I begin this book		On finishing this book	
I rate myself at:	My friend/spouse says:	I rate myself at:	My friend/spouse says:

3. I have an intimate and clear ongoing relationship with God and hear His leadings

As I begin this book		On finishing this book	
I rate myself at:	My friend/spouse says:	I rate myself at:	My friend/spouse says:

4. I find worship and thanksgiving a natural part of my life

As I begin this book		On finishing this book	
I rate myself at:	My friend/spouse says:	I rate myself at:	My friend/spouse says:

5. When I am aware of an area to grow, I am equipped to follow that process

As I begin this book		On finishing this book	
I rate myself at:	My friend/spouse says:	I rate myself at:	My friend/spouse says:

6. I take personal responsibility for my spiritual health and growth.

As I begin this book		On finishing this book	
I rate myself at:	My friend/spouse says:	I rate myself at:	My friend/spouse says:

7. I am aware, and people confirm, that I am growing in my spiritual walk

As I begin this book		On finishing this book	
I rate myself at:	My friend/spouse says:	I rate myself at:	My friend/spouse says:

8. I am secure and at peace with who I am

As I begin this book		On finishing this book	
I rate myself at:	My friend/spouse says:	I rate myself at:	My friend/spouse says:

9. I have control of my inner world and do not feel obliged to sin

As I begin this book		On finishing this book	
I rate myself at:	My friend/spouse says:	I rate myself at:	My friend/spouse says:

10. When God convicts me to change, I recognise His grace to overcome

As I begin this book		On finishing this book	
I rate myself at:	My friend/spouse says:	I rate myself at:	My friend/spouse says:

11. I am not entangled in the priorities of the world or the idols it puts in place of God

As I begin this book		On finishing this book	
I rate myself at:	My friend/spouse says:	I rate myself at:	My friend/spouse says:

12. When God highlights an area of life to change, I know how to plan for growth

As I begin this book		On finishing this book	
I rate myself at:	My friend/spouse says:	I rate myself at:	My friend/spouse says:

PART 2: OUR DAY-TO-DAY STRUGGLES

We all have areas where we are yet to break through. Use this exercise to help you identify them.

Key to answers.

0	1	2
This is not something I experience	I slip in this area occasionally but not regularly	So far I have not been able to overcome this

		0	1	2
1	I struggle with feelings of inadequacy.			
2	I feel a strong burden of having to provide well for my family.			
3	I find myself secretly competing with the people around me.			
4	I tend to build cases against people who seem successful or have power over me.			
5	I spend a lot of time wondering what people think about me.			
6	When people don't agree with me I take it personally and tend to think that they have rejected me.			
7	I am easily offended.			
8	I over-react when I feel judged.			
9	I lash out when my self-worth is threatened.			
10	I'm jealous when my partner talks to the opposite sex.			
11	I control who my partner sees and where they go.			
12	I need to be in a relationship to feel OK.			
13	When I look at myself I am never satisfied.			
14	I struggle with body image.			
15	I hide how much I drink.			
16	I drink to get drunk.			
17	When I drink I always get tipsy or go over-board.			
18	I turn to drugs or medication to ease my inner struggles.			
19	I use food to cope with my feelings.			
20	Sometimes I want to hurt myself.			
21	I struggle with viewing pornography.			
22	I have gay thoughts and feelings.			
23	I have a problem with sex.			
24	I change my opinion to please other people.			
25	I feel compelled to argue with or manipulate people into agreeing with me.			
26	I feel I have been misunderstood most of my life.			
27	Sometimes I hit my partner when I get angry.			
28	I struggle to control my anger with those around me.			

		0	1	2
29	I struggle to form relationships and trust others.			
30	I judge people often and it lessens my view of them.			
31	When I am angry at someone I want to hurt them in some way.			
32	I struggle with fears generally.			
33	I have a fear of rejection.			
34	I worry about the future.			
35	I have a fear of being inadequate or insignificant.			
36	I have a fear of failure.			
37	I often feel like something is about to go wrong.			
38	I overwork and feel really low when I am not accomplishing something.			
39	I am afraid to set goals because when I don't reach them, it makes me feel like I have failed.			
40	People think I am obsessed with being right.			
41	I do not know when to take a rest.			
42	A lot of the time I only feel good if I look my best.			
43	I feel ashamed about things I've done in the past.			
44	I can't forgive myself.			
45	I feel numb or even empty inside.			
46	Nothing I do is ever good enough.			
47	I only feel significant when I'm working.			
48	I only feel good about myself when I have been exercising.			
49	I feel like there's a ceiling between me and God.			
50	I want to win all of the time.			
51	I know what I'm doing is wrong but I can't seem to stop.			
52	I am not able to trust God to do what I need.			
53	I struggle to make decisions without God guiding me explicitly.			
54	I am a different person at home than I am at church, work or school.			
55	I have areas of my life I cannot talk about with anyone.			
56	When people get too close, I withdraw.			
57	I am afraid people will be disappointed if they saw the real me.			
58	I think God is angry with me because of my failures.			

Q. Are there any other areas you would like to be able to address?

_____

_____

Q. If you had to highlight one or two areas to deal with, what would they be?

_____

_____

[1.4]

Afraid and alone

CHAPTER SUMMARY:

- Idols are the things we defer to rather than God.
- They are tangible representations of our slave-drivers.
- Without God, we all suffer from an orphaned spirit.

YOUR RESPONSE:

Look over at this list of common modern-day idols and mark those that you either:
- Consider when making decisions
- Use to feel significant
- Get more passionate or excited about than God
- Use as source of security
- Look to in determining your future direction.

	Sport		Body image	
	Fashion		Appearance	
	Success		Materialism	
	Power		Approval	
	Control		Independence	
	Significance		Individualism	
	Comfort		Money	
	Entitlement		Recognition	

Q. Have another idol in your life? List it here.

_____

_____

_____

OTHER NOTES:

For more in-depth and comprehensive background on idols in our culture, refer to the material by Timothy Keller.

In particular:
- Keller, T. 2010, *The Gospel in Life: Grace Changes Everything*, Zondervan.
- Keller, T. 2011, *Counterfeit Gods*, Penguin Putnam Inc.

[1.5]

Corrupted Comparison

CHAPTER SUMMARY:

- Conceit and ambition are common manifestations of an orphaned spirit.
- They are a reflection of the nature of Satan.
- Ungodly ambition is a self-focused and self-promoting drive to advance in order to find an increased sense of significance.

YOUR RESPONSE:

Q. How does conceit manifest in your life?

_____

_____

_____

_____

_____

_____

_____

_____

OTHER NOTES:

Q. How would you describe your level of ambition to do better in life?

_____

_____

_____

_____

_____

_____

_____

Q. What do you think is driving these issues in you?

_____

_____

_____

_____

_____

_____

_____

[1.6]
Redeemed Hope

CHAPTER SUMMARY:

- We are called to live with a heavenly perspective.
- Hope is based in what can be, and our ability to endure the journey.
- Hope is futile without Christ within giving us what we need.

YOUR RESPONSE:

Q. Considering the various slave drivers and idols brought to your attention this week, how different might the future look for you if God could heal and empower you for freedom?

_____

_____

Q. How would you describe that freedom? Is it a future you would actually prefer?

_____

_____

> **CONCLUSION OF GROUP MEETING 2**
>
> In closing, pray for each other that Christ would give them clarity in their hopes and dreams. Seek God for specific grace to overcome the issues raised through this week's material

Week 2 – What do you want?

Group Session 3

Use this section to introduce your 3rd group meeting.

> **INTRODUCTION**
>
> Holy desire is not a common issue to raise in western churches. And yet it is a fundamental part of kingdom culture that we can only overlook if we are determined to.
>
> Q. What was your over-arching response to the material this week?
>
> _____
>
> _____
>
> _____
>
> _____
>
> _____
>
> _____
>
> Discuss together your responses from this week's teaching:

[2.1]
Out of the box

CHAPTER SUMMARY:

- God has no limits, and His plans for us take the same form.
- Forming a preferred future is hard for many people.
- God wants to get you out of your self-imposed box.

YOUR RESPONSE:

Q. Is there an area of your life where you have lost hope? You can tell, because it will be an area where you don't plan to see change happen. Perhaps it is as little as a way of thinking, or as large as your hopes for calling, happiness and legacy.

Where do you find it hardest to hope?

_____
_____
_____
_____
_____
_____

OTHER NOTES:

[2.2]

The posture of hope

CHAPTER SUMMARY:

- God wants to engage with those who desire Him.
- People can be unwilling; willing, or; wanting to engage with God.
- Your spiritual life is exactly where you want it to be.

YOUR RESPONSE:

Q. How would you describe your level of desire for change or a better future? If you had to rate it on a scale, where is it currently and where do you believe it should be?

_____

_____

_____

_____

_____

_____

_____

_____

_____

[2.3]

Building desire

CHAPTER SUMMARY:

- Desire for God is something that can be grown.
- We are not obliged to the desires of our old nature.
- Our desire for God must be greater than any other desire.

YOUR RESPONSE:

Q. The Psalms are full of David's prayers and desires. If you were to write a note like that to God, what would it be? What are your desires, both good and bad? Spend a few minutes expressing your heart to God about the things that drive so much of your life right now.

_____

_____

_____

_____

_____

_____

_____

_____

[2.4]
Desiring God

CHAPTER SUMMARY:

- It is possible for us to objectify God.
- We are to reflect God's image, not make Him in ours.
- When we desire God, our agendas and wish-lists change.

YOUR RESPONSE:

Q. Consider for a moment the things you pray about – that list you bring to God for Him to address. Could it be that you have looked to Him as the giver of answers more than the lover of your soul? How might you have objectified God?

_____

_____

_____

_____

_____

_____

_____

_____

[2.5]

Desiring freedom

CHAPTER SUMMARY:

- To turn to the Lord means I turn away from relying on my own strength and rely on what He has done for me at the cross.
- Lack of desire to change is the most common reason for being stuck.
- As we come in to line with God's desires, He empowers our choices.

YOUR RESPONSE:

Q. What is clogging your spiritual lungs? Is there a sin you feel obliged to, or a bitterness that you can't let go of? Perhaps you are afraid or addicted to control or comfort or pleasure.

Ask God to reveal to you what is clogging your spiritual lungs.

_____

_____

_____

_____

_____

_____

_____

[2.6]

Creating a hope

CHAPTER SUMMARY:

- God loves it when we initiate a godly dream.
- Godly hopes rely on Him to make it possible.
- A future hope anchors our soul.

YOUR RESPONSE:

Q. Are you able to identify your unacceptable present and your preferred future? Write them down and lay out a dream before God of a life worth fighting for.

_____
_____
_____
_____
_____
_____
_____
_____

CONCLUSION OF GROUP MEETING 3

A preferred future

What are the facets of my current reality that are unacceptable?	What might be the opposite, or preferred alternative?

Share with each other the detail of your dream for a preferred future.

How would your feelings be different?

_____

_____

What habits would change?

_____

_____

What relationships might be altered, ceased or started?

_____

_____

How would you invest you time differently?

_____

_____

In closing, pray for each other that God would stir up and confirm this dream.

Week 3 – Kairos

Group Session 4

Use this section to introduce your 4th group meeting.

INTRODUCTION

Kairos moments are an invitation to come off the path of life that has gotten you to this point, and to grow through a new level of engagement with God.

This week you will have been confronted with a choice: to change or not to change. Your decision will be determined by your desire. What do you want to do? Will you stay the same or will you grow? God leaves that choice in your hands.

Q. How would you describe your desire given what you know now?

_____

_____

_____

RETREAT AND ADVANCE

For participants who attended a spiritual retreat in the last week.

The days following a time of spiritual refreshment can be somewhat difficult to navigate. Disengaging from normality to spend time with God and His people gives a unique and somewhat unsustainable opportunity to extend our hearts in a deliberate mountain-top experience.

Every mountain casts its own shadow. What happens on Monday when we re-engage with the life we left behind? The same people, problems and stresses are waiting for us. Were my gains valid? What if I didn't experience what I was hoping for? All sorts of questions come to mind.

Good! That is what is supposed to happen. Mountain tops give us a new vision for what normal can look like if we grow over time.

It is not practical to breathe the rarified air of the summit indefinitely – and so we must allow ourselves to fall back and recover. To grow in any area, we must extend past our present sustainable limit, then enter a phase of re-creation. There our spirit grows and adapts, ready to extend again.

This is what a "rhythm of grace" is all about!

Q. What questions and thought processes have arisen in response to your spiritual retreat?

[3.1]

What time is it?

CHAPTER SUMMARY:

- Repentance and belief provide the rhythm for transformation.
- Kairos means an *opportune moment*.
- We can bring the power of God's kingdom into these moments.

YOUR RESPONSE:

Q. Write down a short list of the things God has been trying to work out with you for some time. Then, ask God to shine a light on the one issue above all others that he wants to address in this season.

_____

_____

_____

_____

_____

_____

_____

_____

[3.2]

One more night

CHAPTER SUMMARY:

- Avoiding the problem only increases the effect.
- We retain the ability to choose God's way or our own.

YOUR RESPONSE:

Q. What are the frogs that you have avoided dealing with? Think of the idols and slave drivers highlighted so far: what has been attached to that for too long, and needs to be cut off?

_____

_____

_____

_____

_____

_____

_____

_____

[3.3]
Spotting the problem

CHAPTER SUMMARY:

- What seems to be a small issue to us, may not be small in God's sight.
- What we allow, we condone. What we condone will grow.
- God might ask us to deal with an issue, but eventually he will tell us to.

YOUR RESPONSE:

Q. You have already spent time considering your preferred future, and the things you believe God has been working on in your life. Perhaps there are other fruit in your life that do not seem to be connected to those things already listed. Take the time now to write down the recurring issues that, big or small, do not go away.

_____

_____

_____

_____

_____

_____

_____

_____

[3.4]
Approaching the no-go zone

CHAPTER SUMMARY:

- There are issues in our lives that we will avoid at almost any cost.
- The absence of God in that place compels us to replace Him with an idol.
- We form protective strategies to keep this area off-limits.

YOUR RESPONSE:

Q. What are your no-go zones? Why do you think they have been kept off limits for so long?

_____

_____

_____

_____

_____

_____

_____

_____

_____

[3.5]

What is the alternative?

CHAPTER SUMMARY:

- We keep repeating the same behavior if we rely on our own strength.
- Only through God's Spirit can we deal with the state of our heart.

YOUR RESPONSE:

Q. What is on offer for you to replace the issues God is wanting to address? What fruit of the Spirit could overrule the fruit of the old nature? If you could ask God for one thing in this regard, what would it be?

_____

_____

_____

_____

_____

_____

_____

_____

_____

_____

[3.6]

Placing everything on the table

CHAPTER SUMMARY:

- God came to save us as whole-people.
- We must leave the whole-person on the table for transformation.
- A person who wants to be free must have nothing left to hide.

YOUR RESPONSE:

Q. Is there anything you have struggled to put on the table? List it here for your own confession, and ask yourself why it has been so important to you.

_____

_____

_____

Q. Can you honestly say that everything in your life is now on the table?

_____

_____

CONCLUSION OF GROUP MEETING 4

Spend some time praying for each member of the group. Ask God to give them clarity and grace for their next steps in the journey to transformation and spiritual empowerment.

Week 4 – Repent

Group Session 5

Use this section to introduce your 5th group meeting.

INTRODUCTION

This week you have spent time and prayer seeking God for some underlying issues in your life. We all have these dark closets, some of which we didn't even know existed. Some of us have simply thought the closet to be irrelevant or inevitable, and so it has remained taking up space in our life.

The only reason we open those doors is to shine a light and bring redemption. Introspection is something that should be measured and done with a heart to bring change, not sadness.

Q. What was your overall response to the week of teaching on repentance?

_____

_____

_____

_____

_____

[4.1]

A rhythm of grace

CHAPTER SUMMARY:

- Transformation is not about performing at a higher standard.
- God's grace gives us what we need for abundant life.
- We are to walk and work in rhythm.

YOUR RESPONSE:

Q. Where have you experienced spiritual tiredness?

_____

_____

_____

_____

Q. What have been the struggles you are unable to overcome in your own strength?

_____

_____

_____

_____

[4.2]

Repentance

CHAPTER SUMMARY:

- To repent means to turn.
- During repentance we are to confess the problem, coming into agreement with God about it.
- Repentance turns from one thing, and toward another.

YOUR RESPONSE:

Q. In regard to the issue you have chosen to address, what might be the wrong thinking that has led to that being a longstanding part of your life?

_____

_____

_____

_____

Q. What lies might you believe about yourself, or about God?

_____

_____

_____

_____

Q. Where do you need to turn your thinking?

_____
_____
_____
_____
_____
_____

Q. Where have you experienced spiritual tiredness?

_____
_____
_____
_____
_____
_____
_____
_____

[4.3]

Looking behind the idol

CHAPTER SUMMARY:

- Many problems start by trying to meet valid needs in invalid ways.
- Satan offers counterfeits to the ways God meets our needs.
- We need to go deeper than looking at bad fruit, and look for the root.

YOUR RESPONSE:

Q. In chapter 1.4 you identified an idol that you bow to. What is it? Why do you think it has come to have the place in your life that it does? Is there a lie you have believed and need to repent of?

_____

_____

_____

_____

_____

_____

_____

_____

_____

[4.4]

Dishonour

CHAPTER SUMMARY:

- By dishonouring others, we miss out on the rewards that come through that relationship.
- This can begin as a child and go on have ramifications for our whole life.

YOUR RESPONSE:

Q. Perhaps the issue of dishonour is not one that you need to consider. If you have prayed and feel that you hold everyone in the level of regard that God expects, then enjoy the rewards of that. However, if God has raised an issue for you to deal with, write it down here and include your prayerful response in how to deal with it.

_____

_____

_____

_____

_____

_____

_____

_____

[4.5]

Offence

CHAPTER SUMMARY:

- Offence is a result of judgment.
- To be offended causes us to stumble.
- We must clear the scales of judgment.

YOUR RESPONSE:

Q. What has held you back in life, or been the point of restricted blessing?

_____

_____

Q. When you asked God, who did He say that you need to forgive?

_____

_____

Q. Why would that be?

_____

_____

_____

_____

Q. What inner vow might have resulted from your judgments of another?

_____

_____

_____

_____

Q. Are there people or situations you now avoid, or a life path you chose out of spite or rebellion?

_____

_____

_____

_____

_____

_____

_____

_____

[4.6]

Navigating a turn

CHAPTER SUMMARY:

- Repentance requires a commitment to change.
- Elijah had to be prepared to both listen and act.

YOUR RESPONSE:

Q. When determining a preferred future, you do not yet need to know fully how to get there. You can assume that you will need the help of God and His people to go forward. For now, you need to be clear about what thoughts, fears, judgments and inner vows you may need to turn from – and what you want to replace them with. What will you turn from, and where will you turn to?

_____

_____

> ### CONCLUSION OF GROUP MEETING 5
>
> You need God's grace to overcome. We are not designed to live or grow in our own strength; that is why you have found it impossible up until now.
>
> The next week of readings invite you into a journey of faith where you can posture yourself to grasp the elements of kingdom life that meet your needs.
>
> Pray together that each participant will be able to receive the particular grace God has for them.

Week 5 – Believe

Group Session 6

Use this section to introduce your 6th group meeting.

INTRODUCTION

I wonder if this week's material caught you by surprise. When we consider a life of faith, the conversation normally leans towards themes other than personal surrender and experiencing Shalom!

However, because the kingdom is found by engaging with God's Spirit in humility, faith at its best is found this way.

Q. What was your overall response to this week's content?

_____

_____

Your responses from the past week

First read together 2 Peter 1:3–9.

What needs to be added to your life by God for you to transform as you intend?

_____

_____

_____

[5.1]

The kingdom at hand

CHAPTER SUMMARY:

- Faith is a reliance on what we already have, or of God's promise that we will.
- Faith is active reliance rather than theoretical agreement.

YOUR RESPONSE:

Q. Considering the issue in which you want transformation, what element of the kingdom do you need to embrace? What grace do you need from God?

_____

_____

_____

_____

_____

_____

_____

_____

_____

[5.2]

What storm?

CHAPTER SUMMARY:

- God helps us to live above our circumstances.
- We don't always have faith that seas will be calm, but we can have faith to be kept safe within the storm.
- No matter what our circumstance, we are expected to have faith.

YOUR RESPONSE:

Q. Has there been a situation or circumstance that, until now, you have seen as the reason why you cannot break through?

_____

_____

_____

_____

_____

_____

_____

_____

_____

Q. How does this idea of peace in the storm apply to your life?

[5.3]
The rest of faith

CHAPTER SUMMARY:

- Deep faith is to surrender all to God regardless of what will or has happened to us.
- God knows what we need and when we need it – that is His job.
- We find Him most clearly when we come with peace and faith.

YOUR RESPONSE:

Q. What is stopping you from finding peace with God? Is there a prayer that remains unanswered? A situation you expect Him to fix? Will you surrender to God in faith, not needing those things to be solved?

Spend a few minutes now writing out a prayer of surrender to God.

_____

_____

_____

_____

_____

_____

_____

Q. Has there been a situation or circumstance that, until now, you have seen as the reason why you cannot break through?

_____

_____

_____

_____

_____

_____

_____

_____

_____

_____

_____

_____

_____

_____

_____

_____

_____

[5.4]

Pathway to joy

CHAPTER SUMMARY:

- An experience of peace inevitably leads to joy.
- Praise is connected to thanksgiving – worship is connected to sacrifice.

YOUR RESPONSE:

Q. What has been the source of your joy to this point? When has the Lord provided you with the deepest sense of His joy in your life?

_____

_____

_____

_____

_____

_____

_____

_____

_____

[5.5]

The higher calling

CHAPTER SUMMARY:

- Our higher calling is to live from the Spirit.
- As heirs of God, we can live from and grow our spiritual inheritance.

YOUR RESPONSE:

Q. Where has God placed you that requires you to steward that inheritance? Are there people in your family, community or workplace that need you to cover them in prayer?

_____

_____

_____

_____

_____

_____

_____

_____

_____

Q. How could you focus better on growing God's family business?

[5.6]

A point of no return

CHAPTER SUMMARY:

- Faith is at its best when the things we don't understand, don't rob us of what we do understand.
- The journey God calls us to is not absent of pain altogether.
- True steps of faith require us to delete any exit strategy back to our old way of living.

YOUR RESPONSE:

Q. If you have come to a point of wanting to proceed in faith with God in a new way, then spend some time now writing a letter of surrender to God. Tell Him where you are committing to alter your life, and in which areas you need His strength and provision. Then offer yourself to Him as an act of worship.

_____

_____

_____

_____

_____

_____

_____

CONCLUSION OF GROUP MEETING 6

Share together, if appropriate, your letter of surrender to God.

Pray for each other that God would bless each one with new forms of grace for their next steps.

Week 6 – A plan to change

Group Session 7

Use this section to introduce your 7th group meeting.

> **INTRODUCTION**
>
> This course has invited you into a Christ-centred life, rather than a moral-centred life. Some might assume that our personal transformation is all about behaving better. Living morally is a good thing, but it is second prize – one of many second prizes in Christian living.
>
> First prize is deep union with Christ. Live this way and, as Jesus says, the rest comes naturally. Morality is much more of a fruit of our union with Christ than it is a route to that union.
>
> *"But seek first his kingdom and his righteousness, and all these things will be given to you as well".*
> *(Matthew 6:33)*
>
> Q. What was your overall response to this week's content?
>
> _____
> _____
> _____
> _____

[6.1]

What am I aiming for, really?

CHAPTER SUMMARY:

- God longs jealously for your heart.
- He wants to engage with those that want Him.
- God doesn't want what you do, He wants you.

YOUR RESPONSE:

Q. Do you want what Jesus wants? After all you have been reflecting on these last weeks, what is your desire now? Spend some time writing out what you long for in your life with God.

_____

_____

_____

_____

_____

_____

_____

_____

_____

[6.2]

Walking in union

CHAPTER SUMMARY:

- We are called to be at one with God.
- When the world loses its grip on us, we fall in to the arms of people.
- You can only give what you genuinely possess.

YOUR RESPONSE:

Q. Does the picture of life described in this chapter appeal to you? What is the response of your heart to the idea that the well-being of people becomes more of a priority than the agendas of this world?

_____

_____

_____

_____

_____

_____

_____

_____

_____

[6.3]

Heart of flesh; face like flint

CHAPTER SUMMARY:

- We must stay soft to God, and resolute to follow Him.
- An achievable and worthy dream with intentional steps is very motivating.

YOUR RESPONSE:

Q. Today, spend time filling out the first four questions in your Plan to Change

WHAT NEEDS TO CHANGE?

_____

_____

_____

_____

_____

WHY DOES IT NEED TO CHANGE?

_____

_____

_____

WHAT IS THE PROBLEM?

_____

_____

_____

_____

_____

_____

_____

WHAT WILL IT LOOK LIKE WHEN THE CHANGE HAS TAKEN PLACE?

_____

_____

_____

_____

_____

_____

_____

[6.4]

How did Jesus grow people?

CHAPTER SUMMARY:

- To grow we need four dynamics of transformation at work:
    - Spiritual
    - Experiential
    - Relational
    - Instructional

YOUR RESPONSE:

Q. Think of your past experiences of growth in life. Which of the four elements came in to play, and how did they result in transformation?

_____

_____

_____

_____

_____

_____

_____

_____

[6.5]

Form a strategy

CHAPTER SUMMARY:

- The spiritual dynamic connects us to God.
- The experiential dynamic connects us to life.
- The relational dynamic connects us to people.
- The instructional dynamic connects to truth.

YOUR RESPONSE:

Q. Consider the area in which you want to grow, and think through how each dynamic might hold a key for your next stage. These will make up your Plan for Growth.

Spiritual Dynamic – how do I need to connect with God?
Consider ways to engage more vibrantly, praise and worship genuinely, embrace His Spirit more powerfully.
Is there a way to measure progress?

Experiential dynamic – how do I need to connect with life?

Consider new places and practices to engage with that will stretch you where needed.

Is there a way to measure progress?

Relational Dynamic – how do I need to connect with people?

Consider who might be able to support, guide, complement and encourage you.

Is there a way to measure progress?

Instructional Dynamic – how do I need to connect with truth?
Consider what training or teaching would help you understand God, His ways and His grace more fully.
Is there a way to measure progress?

[6.6]

Take a step

CHAPTER SUMMARY:

- It is time to take a step.
- Life will try to drag you back where you were – be ready for that.

YOUR RESPONSE:

Q. What is the step you will take today to initiate your journey into transformation?

_____

_____

Appendix: 1 A Plan to Change

Use this 1-page plan to summarise your next steps.

WHAT NEEDS TO CHANGE?

_____

_____

_____

WHY DOES IT NEED TO CHANGE?

_____

_____

_____

WHAT IS THE PROBLEM?

_____

_____

_____

WHAT WILL IT LOOK LIKE WHEN THE CHANGE HAS TAKEN PLACE?

_____

_____

_____

Spiritual Dynamic – how do I need to connect with God?
I will know I have succeeded when ...

Experiential dynamic – how do I need to connect with life?
I will know I have succeeded when ...

Relational Dynamic – how do I need to connect with people?
I will know I have succeeded when ...

Instructional Dynamic – how do I need to connect with truth?
I will know I have succeeded when ...

Notes from your Retreat

Notes from your Retreat

Notes from your Retreat

Notes from your Retreat

www.ingramcontent.com/pod-product-compliance
Lightning Source LLC
Chambersburg PA
CBHW081421300426
44110CB00017BA/2340